Bones

Injury, Illness and Health

Carol Ballard

Heinemann Library
Chicago, Illinois

Customer Service 888-454-2279

Visit our website at www.heinemannlibrary.com

Originated by Ambassador Litho
Printed and bound in China by South China Printing Company

07 06 05 04 03
10 9 8 7 6 5 4 3 2 1

Library of Congress Cataloging-in-Publication Data
Ballard, Carol
    Bones / Carol Ballard
       v. cm. -- (Body focus)
Summary: The human skeleton -- Healthy bones -- Types of bone -- Bone structure -- Bone marrow -- Broken bones -- Bone diseases -- Different joints -- Inside joints -- Joint problems and injuries -- Knee injuries -- Arthritis -- Joint replacements -- Spine -- Looking after your spine -- Spinal problems and injuries -- Skull - Ribcage -- Arm and hand -- Leg and foot.
Includes bibliographical references and index.
    ISBN 1-4034-0194-2 -- ISBN 1-4034-0450-X (pbk.)
    1. Bones--Juvenile literature. [1. Bones. 2. Skeleton.] I. Title. II. Series.
    QP88.2 .B35 2003
    611'.71--dc21
                              2002014427

Acknowledgments
The author and publishers are grateful to the following for permission to reproduce copyright material:
pp. 5, 42 Science Photo Library/Manfred Kage; p. 6 Imagestate; p. 7 Corbis/Kevin Fleming; pp. 10, 30 Science Photo Library; p. 11 Science Photo Library/BSIP, University of Zurich; p. 12 Science Photo Library/Secchi-Lecaque, CNRI; p. 13 Science Photo Library/Martin Dohrn; pp. 14, 23 Science Photo Library/Department of Clinical Radiology, Salisbury District Hospital; p. 15 Science Photo Library/Damien Lovegrove; p. 16 Science Photo Library/Alfred Pasieka; p. 17 Science Photo Library/Biophoto Associates; p. 20 Science Photo Library/Peter Gardiner; p. 22 Corbis Stockmarket/Tom and Dee Ann McCarthy; p. 25 Corbis Stockmarket/Lester Lefkowitz; pp. 26, 34, 37 Science Photo Library/Dr. P. Marazzi; p. 28 Science Photo Library/Mike Devlin; pp. 29, 35 Science Photo Library/Princess Margaret Rose Orthopaedic Hospital; p. 38 Science Photo Library/Gusto; p. 39 Science Photo Library/Mauro Fermariello; p. 40 Corbis Stockmarket/Phillip Bailey.

Cover photograph of the bones in a healthy human foot reproduced with permission of Science Photo Library.

The publishers would like to thank David Wright for his assistance with the preparation of this book.

Every effort has been made to contact copyright holders of any material reproduced in this book. Any omissions will be rectified in subsequent printings if notice is given to the publishers.

Some words are shown in bold, **like this.** You can find out what they mean by looking in the glossary.

CONTENTS

THE HUMAN SKELETON

The human skeleton provides a strong framework for the rest of the body. It defines our shape, protects important organs, and allows us to move. It also plays an important role in producing blood cells and in storing **minerals** and fats.

The skeleton of a newborn baby may contain 300 or more bones, but many fuse, or join together, during childhood. Most adults' skeletons have 206 bones. The bones range in size from the tiny, delicate bones of the ear to the long, strong **femur** of the thigh. There is also a wide range of bone shapes, including the long bones of the limbs, the short bones of the wrist and ankle joints, the flat bones of the skull, and the irregular bones of the spine and face. The size and shape of each bone reflects its function.

Support and movement

The spine provides a strong, upright central support. The shoulders are attached to the spine by strong muscles, and the **pelvic girdle** is attached directly to the spine. Arms are suspended from the shoulders, and legs are suspended from the pelvic girdle. This arrangement defines our overall shape and the movements that we can make. Bones protect delicate internal organs from injury. The skull protects the brain, the spine protects the **spinal cord,** and the rib cage protects the heart and lungs.

Muscles are attached to bones by strong **tendons.** When muscles contract, bones are pulled into new positions, allowing us to achieve a wide range of movements. Some movements are large, such as the movement of the femur when we walk, while others are small, such as the precise movements of a violinist's fingers.

Joints are the places where the ends of two bones meet. Your skeleton has more than 200 joints. Some joints, like your knees and elbows, allow the bones to move. Strong bands called **ligaments** hold these joints together, controlling the movement of the bones. Other joints, like those in your skull, are fixed, so the bones cannot move at all.

At the center of some bones is spongy **tissue** called red **bone marrow** that produces some blood cells. Adult bones also contain yellow bone marrow tissue. If we eat more fat than our bodies need, the excess will be transported by the blood to places where it can be stored. Some fat may be stored in the yellow bone marrow and then released when other parts of the body need it. Bone tissue stores minerals, especially calcium and phosphorus, that help to make the bones strong. When these minerals are needed, bones can release them into the bloodstream for transport to other parts of the body.

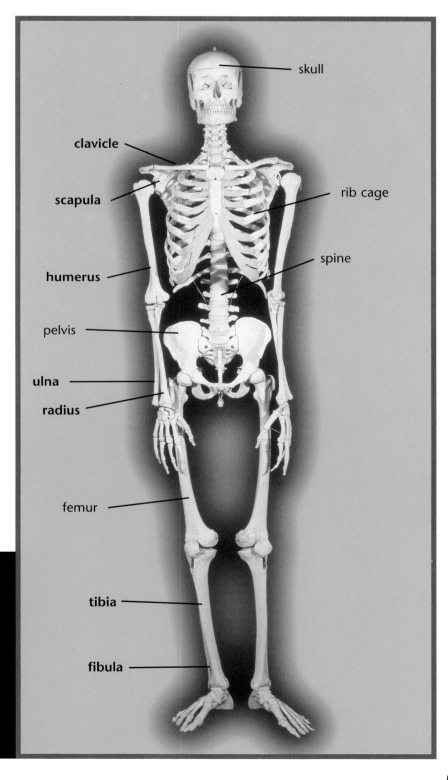

skull

clavicle

scapula

rib cage

spine

humerus

pelvis

ulna

radius

femur

tibia

fibula

This diagram shows the main bones of the human skeleton. You can see how the spine provides a central support for all the bones of the upper body, and the pelvic girdle acts as a frame for the legs to hang and move freely.

HEALTHY BONES

We need to make sure that we take care of our bones, because a strong, healthy skeleton is important if we are to lead active lives. The foods we eat and the amount of exercise we do can both affect our bones.

Diet

Our bones are made from the chemicals that we receive from our food. For bones to grow strong and healthy, we need to make sure that the food we eat provides all the chemicals that our bones need.

Bones contain a lot of calcium and phosphorus, so it is important that your diet contains plenty of these two **minerals**, especially while you are growing. Smaller amounts of other minerals such as fluoride, manganese, iron, and magnesium are also needed. Good sources of calcium include dairy products such as milk and cheese, green vegetables such as broccoli and spinach, and shellfish. Foods rich in phosphorus include dairy products, meat, fish, beans, grains, and eggs. These foods also contain plenty of the other minerals needed.

Some **vitamins** are essential for building strong bones, too. Vitamin D, found in fish oils, butter, and eggs—and also formed by the action of sunlight on skin—is needed to help calcium build up in the bones. Vitamin C, found in most fruits and vegetables but especially in citrus fruits like oranges, also plays an important part in building strong bones.

Dairy products are a good source of calcium and phosphorus, a mineral also found in eggs. Both of these minerals help keep our bones healthy.

Exercise

When you exercise, your bones have to move and support your body's weight. This helps them to become stronger as more minerals are accumulated. Being inactive can cause bones to become weaker, as minerals are lost and bone **tissue** is broken down. The main work our bones do is mechanical, being pulled by muscles when we move and supporting our body against the pull of gravity. Weight-bearing activities such as walking and moderate weightlifting help to build and retain bone **mass**. It is important when you are a teenager to build up as much bone mass as you can. As people age, bone mass is lost and cannot be regained—so the more you have to begin with, the better!

If you are playing a sport where you might injure a bone, try to protect yourself by wearing the correct protective clothing. These football players are likely to suffer less damage beneath all this padding.

Astronauts and bones

Scientists have discovered just how important exercise is for healthy bones by studying what happens to the bones of astronauts who spend a long time in space. Without the pull of gravity, the human body is lighter—this means that the bones do not have to work as hard when exercising. The bones begin to lose calcium and other minerals, and even taking supplements cannot make up for this loss.

Protection

Bones can repair themselves, but it makes much more sense to avoid damaging them in the first place! Many sports activities have protective clothing that is specially designed to protect bones—shin pads for hockey, football, and soccer; helmets for cycling, horseback riding, and mountaineering; and elbow pads and knee pads for inline skating. Players of rough contact sports are extremely well padded and protected.

TYPES OF BONE

The shape and size of bones varies depending on their functions within the body. Large, strong bones like the **femur** are needed for supporting the weight of the body, while smaller, delicate bones such as those inside the ear carry out tiny, precise movements. Bones are usually grouped according to their shape.

Long bones

Long bones are longer than they are wide. They usually have a slight curve that makes them stronger than they would be if they were perfectly straight. There are special places on the long bones where muscles are attached. The bones act as levers, moving when they are

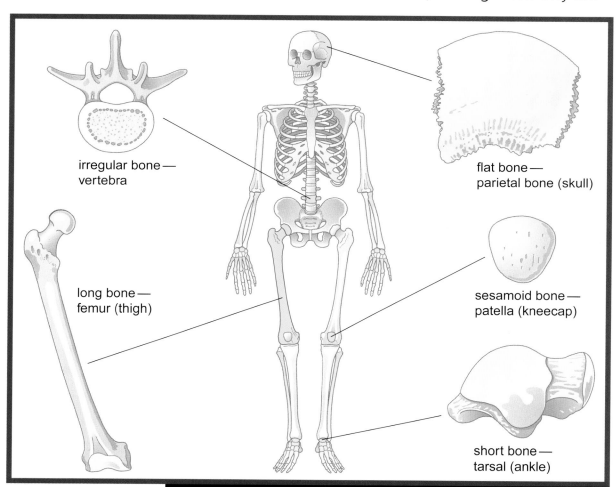

irregular bone —
vertebra

long bone —
femur (thigh)

flat bone —
parietal bone (skull)

sesamoid bone —
patella (kneecap)

short bone —
tarsal (ankle)

These diagrams show some of the main types of bones that make up the human skeleton. A bone's shape is determined by its function. For instance, the bones of the spine must surround and protect the spinal cord, so they fit together tightly and have a hollow center. The femur must support the weight of the body, so it is long and strong.

pulled by the contraction of muscles. The **femur** and **humerus** are examples of long bones.

Short bones

Short bones are roughly cube-shaped—their length, width, and height are almost equal. **Carpals** are short bones found in the joints of the wrists, and **tarsals** are short bones found in the joints of the ankles. These bones allow flexibility as they slide easily past each other.

Flat bones

Flat bones are thin, curved, and strong. Their strength makes them ideal for forming spaces to protect organs. Examples of flat bones are the ribs, **scapulae, sternum**, and some bones of the skull.

Irregular bones

Irregular bones are complex shapes that do not fit into any of the other groups. The **vertebrae** and facial bones are all irregular bones. They have strange parts jutting out from them that allow them to connect with muscles and other bones.

Sesamoid bones

Sesamoid bones get their name because they are the shape of sesame seeds, although they are a lot bigger. They are found in joints where there is **friction** and tension between **tendons** and bones, such as the palms of the hands and soles of the feet. The number of these small bones varies from person to person, but everybody has the two large sesamoid bones that we call the kneecaps **(patellae).**

Accessory bones

Accessory bones are small, extra bones that occur in some people, most often in the feet. They arise when developing bones do not fuse, or join together, completely to make a single bone, so they can look like broken bones on X-rays. This can make it very difficult for doctors to accurately diagnose injuries to bones in the feet. Sutural bones are accessory bones found between the joints of the bones in the skull. When a baby is born, the skull bones are separate, like jigsaw pieces that are not fully connected. As the baby grows, these bones slowly fuse to make the strong dome that we call the **cranium.** The joins between the bones are called sutures, and small sutural bones may be present between the sutures. Because the skull bones do not always fuse together in exactly the same way, the number of sutural bones can vary from one person to another.

Bones are not simple solids. They are made of living **tissue** arranged into several different layers with nerves and a blood supply. Their structure gives them strength while keeping them as light as possible.

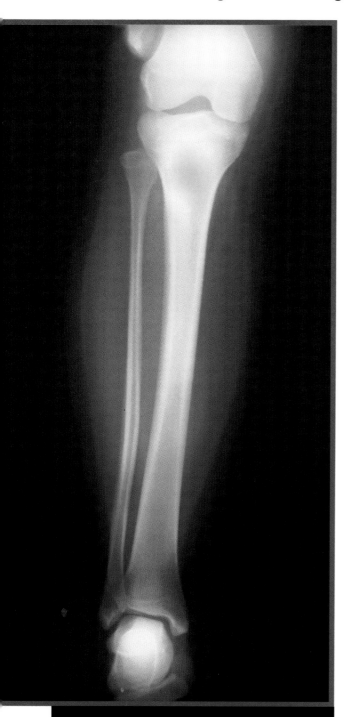

This X-ray shows the two long bones of the lower leg—the **tibia** and **fibula**.

Approximately 70 percent of bone material is made up of different **minerals,** including calcium phosphate and calcium carbonate. The rest of the bone material is a network of living fibers and bone cells. It is the mineral content of the bone that makes it rigid. A baby's bones are quite soft, and young children's bones are still slightly flexible. As people grow older, more calcium from the food they eat is added to the bone structure, and the bones slowly become more rigid.

Types of bone cells

There are three main types of bone cells:
- **Osteocytes** transport nutrients, waste, and gases to and from the blood vessels.
- **Osteoblasts** make new bone tissue so that bones can grow and damage can be repaired.
- **Osteoclasts** break down old bone tissue to release minerals.

The actions of these cells are finely balanced. To maintain healthy bones, it is important that bone tissue is not broken down faster than new bone is produced.

Inside bones

If you look at the inside of a long bone such as the **femur,** you can see several different areas. The long, cylindrical central part is the shaft, or diaphysis. At each end of the shaft is a growth plate, where osteoblasts make new bone tissue, helping the bone grow longer. The outer ends of the bone are covered in a layer of smooth **cartilage,** allowing the bone to move freely at the joint.

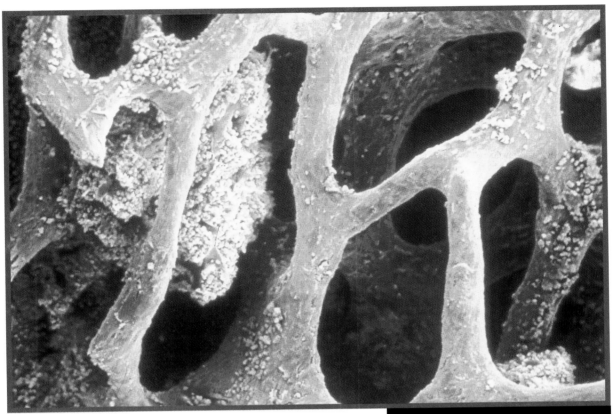

The outer covering of a bone, the periosteum, is a tough, fibrous **membrane.** It contains osteoblasts, and blood vessels and nerves run through it.

Spongy bone has a meshlike structure that makes it strong and supportive.

Inside the periosteum is a layer of dense **compact bone,** similar to the ivory of elephants' tusks. It is a network of bony columns, arranged around central canals that have arteries and veins running through them.

The center of most bones is a light material called **spongy bone,** arranged as a network of thin bars. These run in many different directions, forming a three-dimensional mesh. The large spaces between the bars may be filled with jellylike material called **bone marrow.** Red bone marrow is found at the ends of long bones such as the femur and is involved in the production of red blood cells. Yellow bone marrow fills the spaces in the shafts of long bones, and is mainly fat.

The internal structures of most bones are basically similar, but there are some differences. In some skull bones, there is no spongy bone, just a series of empty spaces called **sinuses.** Flat bones like those in the **cranium** have two thin plates of compact bone with spongy bone sandwiched between them. Irregular bones and short bones have varying amounts of spongy and compact bone.

Red **bone marrow** produces all of the red blood cells and some of the white blood cells in the body. Yellow bone marrow is made up mainly of fat cells. When a baby is born, all of its bones contain red marrow. By the time a person is six or seven years old, some of the red marrow becomes yellow marrow. This process continues until—in most adults—red marrow is found only at the ends of the long bones such as the **femur**, in flat bones such as the ribs and **sternum,** and in the **pelvic girdle.**

Blood cell production

Blood cells age and are broken down, so new ones have to be made continually to replace them. Red bone marrow contains special "stem" cells, a kind of blank cells that can become any of the different types of blood cells. As the stem cells grow and divide, they change and develop, becoming more and more specialized at each stage, until they eventually become new blood cells. Both white blood cells (which are involved in the body's **immune system)** and red blood cells (which transport oxygen around the body) are produced by bone marrow.

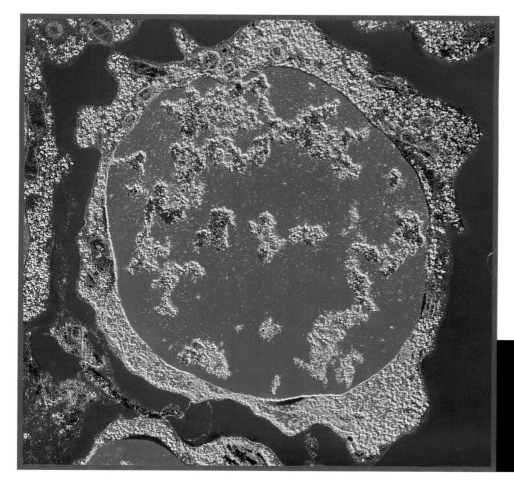

This picture shows a red blood cell forming from human bone marrow.

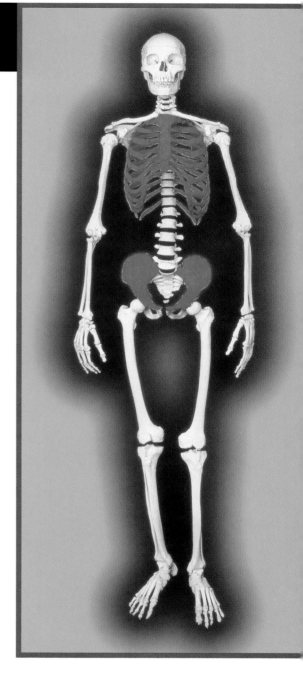

In this picture, the red areas show some of the places where red bone marrow is located in adults.

Red blood cells live for about 120 days. Healthy adults have about 250 million red blood cells in every drop of blood. To maintain this concentration, the bone marrow has to produce at least two million new red blood cells every second!

Control of blood cell production

Blood cell production is controlled by a feedback loop. Red blood cells carry oxygen around the body. If there are too few red blood cells, the level of oxygen in the blood drops. The kidneys detect this drop and release a **hormone** called erythropoietin. This travels around the body in the blood, and when it reaches the bone marrow it speeds up the production of red blood cells. When the oxygen level gets back to normal, the kidneys stop releasing erythropoietin, and red blood cell production slows down again.

Bone marrow problems

There are a number of possible reasons why bone marrow may not produce blood cells properly:

- Some children are born with defective bone marrow.
- Some chemicals can damage bone marrow. These include lead (found in water in buildings with old lead pipes, and in the air in areas with high levels of air pollution), benzene (found in some dyes and fuels), and arsenic (a poisonous chemical sometimes used in pesticides).
- X-rays and other types of radiation damage bone marrow.
- Some types of leukemia (a bone marrow disease) can clog up the bone marrow with malformed white blood cells.

A bone marrow transplant can help in some of these cases. Red bone marrow from a healthy donor is injected into the patient's bloodstream. The stem cells travel around in the blood until they reach the patient's bone marrow. They settle there and begin to produce healthy blood cells. However, it is often difficult to find a suitable donor.

BROKEN BONES

Bones are strong, but an accident such as an awkward fall can break them. The medical term for a broken bone is a **fracture.** Some are simple and mend easily, while others are more complicated and may need surgery to help to repair them.

Type of fracture	What happens to the bone?
greenstick fracture	The bone is partly broken but the rest of it may simply bend like a green tree branch. This occurs mainly in young children because their bones are more flexible than adults' bones.
incomplete fracture	The bone does not break completely into separate pieces. This is sometimes called a hairline fracture.
stress fracture	The bone develops a single crack or a mass of many tiny cracks, without any other damage.
chip	A small piece of bone breaks off of the main bone.
simple fracture	The bone snaps into two pieces, but they stay hidden inside the skin.
compound fracture	This is like a simple fracture, but one or both of the broken ends of the bone stick out through the skin.
comminuted fracture	When the bone breaks, part of it is shattered or crushed into smaller fragments.
impacted fracture	The bone breaks into two pieces, and one is forced a little way into the other.

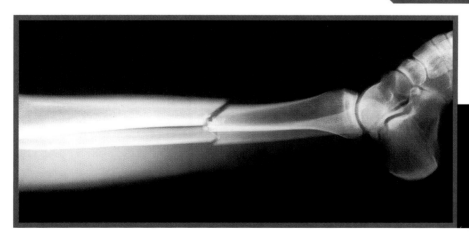

This X-ray shows a multiple fracture to the lower leg. Both the **tibia** and **fibula** have been broken.

Sports-related fractures

One of the bones most commonly fractured by athletes is the **clavicle.** It is often damaged as the result of a clumsy fall. Landing on an arm stretched out to save yourself can put huge pressure on the collarbone, snapping it in two.

Stress fractures are the result of an action being repeated over and over again, such as the thumping of feet on a hard track by runners and jumpers. Wearing training shoes with good support can help to prevent stress fractures.

Treating fractures

To prevent any further damage, broken bones need to be kept as still as possible. A sling can support a broken arm, and **splints** can keep a broken leg rigid. X-rays give more accurate information about the fracture. If it is a simple fracture, wet plaster bandages are wrapped around the bone, drying and hardening to form a protective shell, or cast. Bones that have moved out of alignment need to be repositioned, and some complicated fractures may need surgery to insert metal pins for extra strength.

How bones heal

When a bone is broken, red blood cells pour out from the damaged blood vessels, forming a blood clot at the site of the break. Tiny blood vessels called capillaries slowly grow into the clot, and dead and damaged bone **tissue** is removed by white blood cells and **osteoclasts.** Strong fibers form, connecting the ends of the bone. **Cartilage** forms in between, and the **osteoblasts** gradually make new **spongy bone** tissue. **Compact bone** then forms around the new spongy bone. This whole process may take several months.

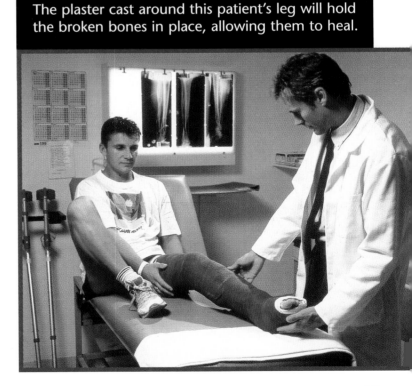

The plaster cast around this patient's leg will hold the broken bones in place, allowing them to heal.

BONE DISEASES

Although our bones are usually strong and healthy, there are various diseases that can affect them. Some are more serious than others. Different diseases affect people of different ages and have different causes, so different treatments are required.

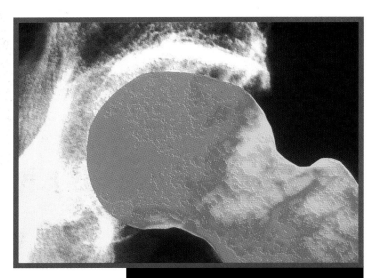

This colored X-ray shows the upper part of a **femur** affected by osteoporosis. The parts colored yellow orange are fractures.

Osteoporosis

Osteoporosis is the weakening of bones as we age. The amount of **minerals** in our bones gradually decreases, and bone **tissue** is broken down more quickly than new tissue is made. The bars of the **spongy bone** become weakened, making the bones brittle and more likely to break. **Fractures** can occur even from normal daily activities—we may say that an older person has fallen and broken a hip, but it is likely that the hip bone fractured and caused the fall. Osteoporosis can be a painful condition, also causing hunching of the backbone and shrinkage.

Osteoporosis causes more problems in women than in men, since their process of bone breakdown begins much earlier. In women, osteoporosis can start sometime after the age of 30 and accelerate in later middle age, when the levels of **hormones** that help to maintain bone strength decrease. Because hormone levels remain at a higher level for longer in men than in women, osteoporosis does not usually begin in men until after the age of 60. Hormone replacement therapy (HRT) and calcium supplements can help to prevent osteoporosis. A diet rich in **vitamins** and minerals—particularly calcium and phosphorus—can reduce a person's risk of developing the disease. Weight-bearing exercise, such as walking, also plays an important role by stimulating the production of more new bone tissue.

Osteomyelitis

Bones can be infected by **microorganisms,** such as *Streptococcus aureus.* **Bacteria** can get into the bone from outside the body when a bone is broken, through a wound, or during surgery. They can also spread inside the body from other infected places, like **abscesses** in the teeth. Infections in bones are called osteomyelitis and can cause fever, sweating, and illness. There may be pus and swelling at the site of infection. Osteomyelitis is usually treated successfully with **antibiotics.**

Rickets and osteomalacia

Vitamin D is needed for calcium to be absorbed in bones as they grow. Without vitamin D, calcium does not accumulate, and the bones become soft and rubbery. This can lead to a disease called rickets, in which a child's bones are too weak to grow properly. The leg bones are not strong enough to carry the weight of the body, so they are bent and bowed. Rickets is much less common in developed countries than it was in the past because diet and living conditions have greatly improved. In adults, lack of vitamin D prevents new bone tissue from being made, and the bones feel painful and tender. This is adult rickets, also called osteomalacia.

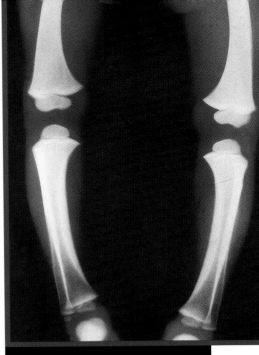

This X-ray shows the bending of the leg bones that is typical in a child suffering from rickets.

Bone tumors

Bones may have odd lumps that do no harm at all, but **tumors** can also develop in bones. Although all bone tumors need to be investigated and treated, many are not **cancerous.** Osteosarcomas are the most common type of bone cancer, and although they may affect older people, they usually occur in people between ten and twenty years old. They can occur in any part of the body but are usually found at the ends of the leg bones or ribs. The area may be painful, but often there are no symptoms, and the disease may be discovered only when the bone breaks at the site of the tumor.

Osteosarcomas can be removed surgically, and afterward the patient usually receives chemotherapy (drug treatment) to kill any remaining tumor cells. Recent advances in treatment mean that these tumors can now usually be completely cured.

Inherited diseases

Some children are born with "brittle bone disease" *(osteogenesis imperfecta).* The bones do not contain enough **proteins** and minerals, so they are very weak and snap easily. Some babies even have broken bones when they are born. These children need to be very careful and be protected from any situations where the bones may be put under strain. This means they are very limited in what they can do, but the bones gradually get stronger as they grow older, and they are more able to lead a normal, active life.

DIFFERENT JOINTS

Joints are the places where two bones meet. They allow the bones to move freely past each other, letting us move all the parts of our bodies. Different types of joints allow different movements. Two of the main types of joints in the human skeleton are hinge joints and ball-and-socket joints.

Hinge joints

You can move a door backward and forward, but you can't move it up and down or around and around. The same is true of hinge joints like the elbow joint. If you keep your upper arm completely still, you can move your lower arm up and down, but you can't wiggle it from side to side or move it around in a circle. The knee is also a hinge joint.

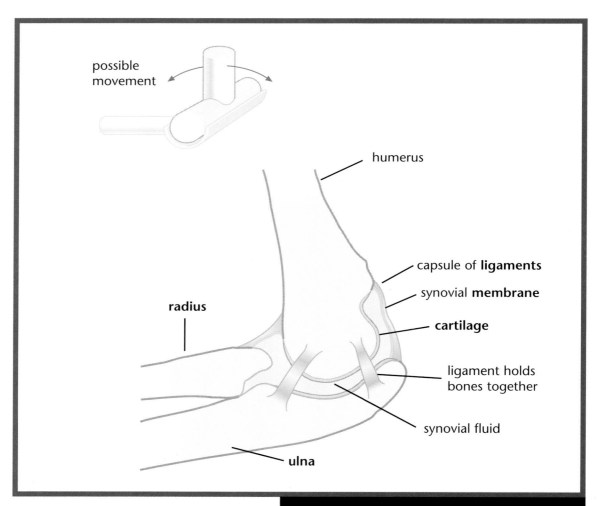

The hinge joint of the elbow allows the lower arm to move up and down.

Ball-and-socket joints

These allow a much wider range of movements than hinge joints. The end of one bone is a round lump (the ball) that fits snugly into a curved space (the socket) in the other bone. The shoulder joint, where the end of the **humerus** fits into the shoulder blade, is a ball-and-socket joint. Because of its design, you have a fuller range of movements—you can move your upper arm in just about any direction you want.

The body's other major ball-and-socket joint is the hip joint, where the ball of the **femur** fits into the socket of the pelvis. Although the bones could move very freely, tough bands of fibers limit their movements, so for most people, the hip joint has a smaller range of movements than the shoulder joint.

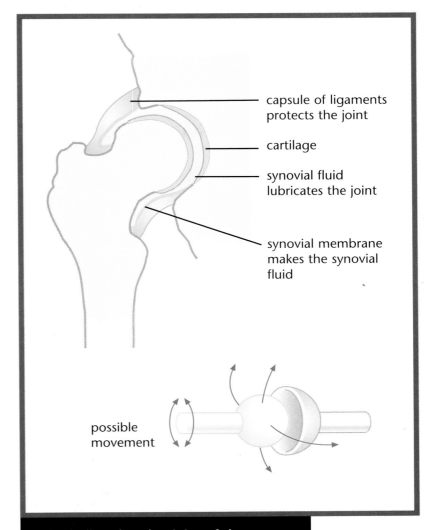

capsule of ligaments protects the joint

cartilage

synovial fluid lubricates the joint

synovial membrane makes the synovial fluid

possible movement

The ball-and-socket joint of the shoulder allows the upper arm to move freely in most directions.

Other joints

Not all our joints follow these two designs. Other types of joints include:

- Fixed joints are found between the bones of the skull. The bones are knitted tightly together, allowing no movement
- Gliding joints of the wrists, ankles, and **vertebrae** allow one bone to glide smoothly over the surface of another.
- Condyloid joints of the wrists and knuckles allow movement both up and down and from side to side.
- Saddle joints between the thumb bones and the wrist bones allow the thumbs to move in all directions.
- Pivot joints allow a rotating movement of one bone around part of another. This type of joint in the neck lets us turn our head from side to side—the top, ring-shaped vertebra balances on a point of the second vertebra.

INSIDE JOINTS

Even the smallest joints are complex constructions. Special structures are needed to hold the bones in place, to keep the ends of the bones from being damaged, and to ensure smooth movements.

Fixed joints

In some fixed joints, bones are knitted together tightly by strong fibers, preventing movement. The bones of the skull are joined in this way. Joints can also be held together tightly by pieces of **cartilage.** These can be found at the joints between the ribs and the **sternum,** and also where bones join at the front of the **pelvic girdle.**

Moving joints

Joints that allow bone movement have a more complex structure than fixed joints, and are called "synovial joints." The ends of each bone are covered with a layer of smooth cartilage to reduce **friction** between them as they move past each other. The cartilage also acts as a cushion, absorbing shock.

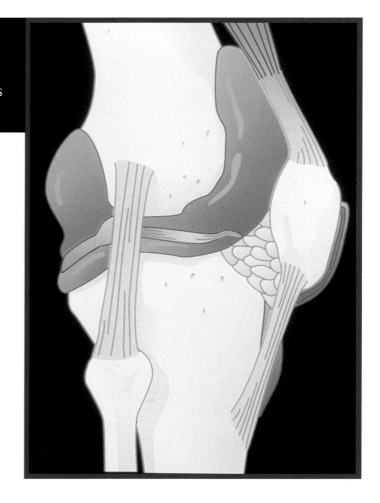

This diagram shows the structures inside a synovial joint—in this case, the knee joint. You can see how the space between the bones is filled with synovial fluid (blue).

The whole joint is surrounded by the articular capsule, a sleevelike cover that links the bones together. The outer layer of the capsule is made of tough fibers that are flexible enough to allow movement but difficult to stretch—preventing the bones from moving out of position. The inner layer, the synovial **membrane,** makes a liquid called synovial fluid. This fluid fills the space between the bones (the synovial cavity) and lubricates the inside surfaces of the joint.

Ligaments

Ligaments are tough bands of fiber that hold joints together. They are really part of the articular capsule and must be very strong to keep the joint from being strained. Some ligaments are tiny, but others are much larger and have their own names. The hip joint has to bear the body's full weight, so the ligaments that hold the ball of the **femur** in its pelvic socket are extremely strong.

Extra structures

Some synovial joints contain other structures in addition to these major ones. Extra bands called accessory ligaments can help to hold a joint together and are important in the knee joint. Some joints have small fluid-filled sacs or pads called **bursae** to act as cushions when a **tendon,** muscle, or skin may rub over a bone.

Some synovial membranes contain fat pads, as in the knee joint. Disks of cartilage may lie between the bones, attached to the articular capsules, where they help to maintain the stability of the joint.

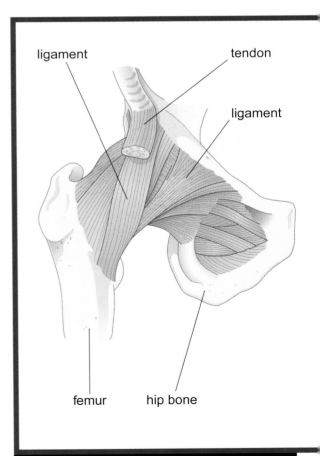

This diagram shows some of the ligaments that hold the hip joint together.

JOINT PROBLEMS AND INJURIES

Joints are complicated structures that allow us to move our bodies in many different ways. They are designed to be strong and stand up to normal wear and tear—but moving bones too far, too fast, or in the wrong direction can damage the joints and cause a variety of injuries.

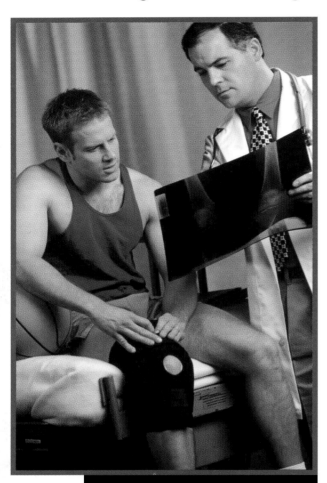

This doctor and athlete are looking at an X-ray of the athlete's knee injury and discussing possible treatments.

Sprain

Sprains are common injuries, caused by wrenching or twisting a joint too far. When **ligaments** are overstressed, they may become stretched or even torn. The joint may swell, and a bruise may develop as blood leaks out of damaged blood vessels around the injury. Sprains can be very painful, but they usually heal by themselves after a while.

You should have a doctor check out any injury, but there are several ways that you can help to relieve the pain of a sprain. You just need to remember the word "RICE." This stands for "Rest, Ice, Compression, and Elevation"—the four main ways to treat injuries like sprains.

Dislocation

Dislocation occurs when the two bones of a joint become separated. The most commonly dislocated joint is the shoulder, when the head of the **humerus** moves out of the socket of the shoulder blade. Usually the humerus moves in front of the shoulder blade instead of behind it.

This injury can be the result of an awkward fall, often in a physical sport such as football. Skilled medical staff can manipulate the joint and push the humerus back into its correct position. An X-ray may be taken to make sure that there are no **fractures.** After dislocation, it is very important to rest the joint in order to give it a chance to heal fully.

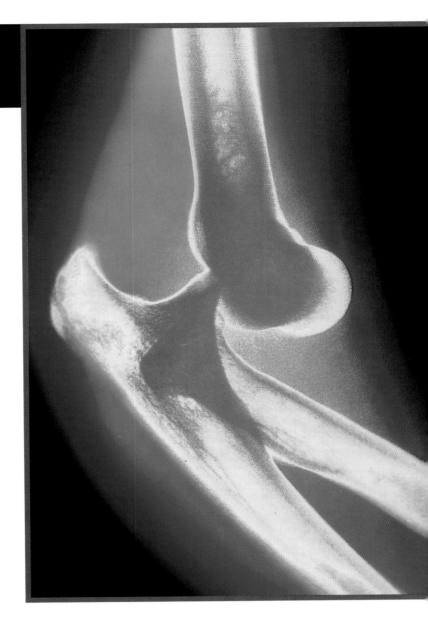

Inflammation

Repeated, vigorous movements can lead to **inflammation** of the **bursae** inside a joint. The joint can become swollen as fluid collects inside it, and movement may be painful and limited. Injuries of this sort are often given names that reflect the type of activity that caused them—for example, "tennis elbow," resulting from overuse of the elbow joint, and "housemaid's knee," from kneeling for long periods.

Injuries like these will heal naturally if the joint is rested. An ice pack can help the inflammation to subside, and anti-inflammatory injections may also help. The extra fluid will drain away slowly, and the swelling will go down, so that movement is possible again.

Joint injuries and sports

Injuries to joints can prevent sporting activities for a while. However frustrating it may be, it makes sense to follow the doctor's advice and not start training again too soon, in order to give the joint time to heal properly. Stretched and torn ligaments take time to heal, dislocated bones need time to settle back into place, and inflammation takes time to subside for any damaged tissue to heal. If you are impatient and use the joint again too soon, you risk aggravating the injury and needing even more time away from training.

KNEE INJURIES

The knee joint is the largest and most complex joint in the body. It is designed to allow the leg to bend, but it also needs to be rigid enough to hold the body stable when we stand still. It can be injured in a variety of ways, and the damage can involve the bones themselves, the **ligaments**, the **cartilage**, and the **tendons** of the joint.

The knee joint

Three bones meet at the knee joint—the **femur, tibia,** and **patella.** Ligaments also link the **fibula** to the knee joint. The end of each bone is covered with a protective layer of cartilage, and pads of cartilage lie between the bones, acting as shock absorbers. Several **bursae** also cushion the knee joint.

Four strong ligaments bind the bones together: two cruciate ligaments make an X shape as they cross over each other, and two collateral ligaments run down the sides of the knee joint. The patella is held in place by the muscles and tendons of the leg.

Torn cartilage

The pads of cartilage inside the joint may be damaged if the knee receives a direct blow or is twisted awkwardly. If cartilage becomes wedged between the bones, the joint may "lock," causing a lot of pain. Doctors may remove small pieces of cartilage that have broken off the main cartilage, or they may remove badly damaged cartilage entirely.

Torn ligaments

Ligaments may be torn by sudden twisting or by a direct blow, as in a football tackle or hockey check. The person may hear a popping sound, and the leg may buckle under his or her weight.

If the ligament is damaged but not completely torn, a protective brace

Inside knees

Until recent years, doctors had no easy way of finding out the extent of damage that may have occurred inside a knee joint. In the 1970s, Japanese surgeons developed the arthroscope, a small, illuminated tube that can be inserted into the knee through a small cut. This provides a clear view of the inside of the knee, sending detailed pictures to a monitor. Doctors can also now use microsurgical operating techniques, often needing a cut less than 0.4 inch (1 centimeter) long and requiring just a single stitch! This means that the recovery time from knee operations is much shorter than it used to be.

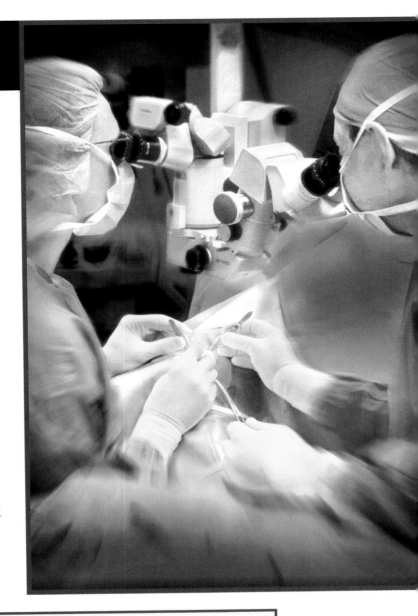

This picture shows a surgeon operating on a patient's knee.

may be worn and exercises prescribed to strengthen the surrounding muscles.

If the ligament is completely torn, it can usually be repaired surgically. Collateral ligaments can be re-attached to the bones. Cruciate ligaments can be attached to sutures (strong threads) that are then threaded through specially drilled holes in the femur, and the ends tied to hold them in place. Doctors may also use pieces of ligaments from elsewhere in the body to help them repair these ligaments. Research is being conducted to try to find the best material to make artificial ligaments. Several, including Gore-Tex, Dacron, and carbon fiber have been tried, but with very limited success.

"Runner's knee"

This is one of the most common knee problems for runners, especially those who run on hills or go long distances. It may be caused by running on an uneven surface, overuse, shoes that do not give enough support, or not enough warm-up. In normal movement, the patella slides backward and forward, but in "runner's knee" it moves sideways a little as well, causing aching and tenderness underneath the patella. The pain usually gets worse when the person walks down stairs, squats down, or sits for a long time. Rest and use of a brace may help to relieve the condition.

Arthritis is the name given to painful, swollen joints. It can have many different causes, but in most cases arthritis falls into one of two main types.

Osteoarthritis

Osteoarthritis occurs when the **cartilage** in the joints wears away. When you move your joints, some of the cartilage at the ends of the bones is worn. Normally, the body replaces the cartilage, but sometimes it is worn away more quickly than the body can replace it. Eventually, the bone surfaces become exposed, and the joint becomes very painful. Large weight-bearing joints like the hip and knee are particularly likely to be affected.

Rheumatoid arthritis

While osteoarthritis is a result of wear on the joints, the causes of rheumatoid arthritis are more complex. It is probably caused by an "autoimmune response." This means that the body's **immune system**, instead of attacking germs from outside the body, attacks its own tissue—in this case, the synovial **membranes** in the body's joints. The cartilage becomes very soft and wears away quickly in many joints throughout the body at the same time.

Who is affected?

Many people believe that only older people are affected by arthritis, but this is not completely true. Osteoarthritis does seem to be a natural product of the aging process, but there are other causes, too. Research has suggested that this arthritis may be linked to certain **genes**, meaning that some people are born with a higher risk of suffering from arthritis than others.

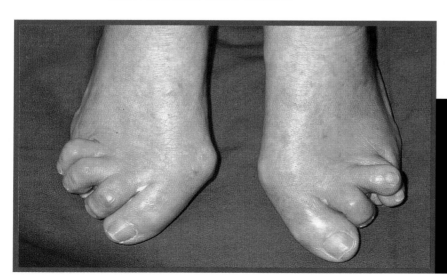

This photograph shows one kind of damage caused by arthritis. Standing and walking must be very painful for this person.

Rheumatoid arthritis, on the other hand, normally starts to show itself between the ages of 20 and 50, with women more likely to be affected than men. There is even a form of rheumatoid arthritis that appears in very young children, between the ages of two and five.

Dealing with arthritis

In most cases, treatment of arthritis is done by relieving the symptoms. One method is to take anti-inflammatory drugs to reduce the **inflammation** inside the joints. Medication is normally part of a three-step treatment that also includes rest (to allow joints to reduce inflammation) and exercise (to rebuild strength in the joint). **Occupational therapists** can help people to find easier ways of doing normal activities so they can avoid using painful joints. In extreme cases of arthritis, doctors can sometimes replace the affected joints.

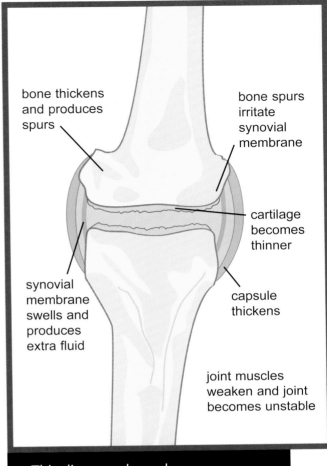

bone thickens and produces spurs

bone spurs irritate synovial membrane

cartilage becomes thinner

synovial membrane swells and produces extra fluid

capsule thickens

joint muscles weaken and joint becomes unstable

This diagram shows how osteoarthritis affects a knee joint.

Gold cure?

In the early part of the twentieth century, scientists discovered that compounds of gold, whether swallowed or injected, could block the immune system and might therefore be an effective treatment for rheumatoid arthritis. However, this treatment has harmful side effects, especially for the kidneys, so it is now used with great caution.

Arthritis and sports

Osteoarthritis can affect younger people, especially if joints are overexercised. There are many cases of professional athletes who have suffered from the condition because they have continued to play even when injured. Anesthetic sprays and creams keep messages from traveling from sensory receptors to the brain. This takes away the immediate pain of an injury so the person can continue to play, but the injury itself may actually be getting worse and worse. Use of **steroids** has also been linked to the development of arthritis at a young age.

JOINT REPLACEMENTS

Modern advances in medicine allow doctors to replace some damaged and worn-out joints with artificial ones. These replacements give patients freedom from pain and allow them to live more active lives than they otherwise could.

Damaged joints

The most common reason for replacement of a joint is osteoarthritis. The **cartilage** covering the ends of the bones wears away, and the bones rub against each other, causing pain when the joint is moved. The most common joint to be replaced is the hip joint. Knees are less commonly replaced, and—although it is possible—shoulder replacement is a relatively unusual operation.

This picture shows an artificial hip joint. The long shaft is inserted into a hole in the femur, and the socket is attached to the pelvis.

History

Doctors have tried for many years to find a way of replacing joints that were damaged or worn out. Eighteenth-century German doctors carried out some of the first experiments, using ivory, but these were not successful. In the twentieth century, more attempts were made, and eventually a British **orthopedic** surgeon, Sir John Charnley, made a breakthrough in the late 1960s. He designed and used a metal ball and a plastic socket for a new hip joint, fastening the pieces in place with a plastic cement that was usually used by dentists. After his pioneering work, many other surgeons refined and perfected the techniques, and now more than 80,000 hip joints are replaced every year in the United States alone.

New developments

Not only have there been developments in surgical techniques used in joint replacement, but the materials used for the replacement parts have changed as well. Some surgeons now use the metal titanium for parts of the new joints. Titanium is more flexible and can support even greater loads than the natural bone. Another new development is an artificial knee joint covered with beads of cobalt. These beads encourage new bone material to grow over the joint, making it stronger and more permanent than just using cement.

Replacing a hip joint

There are two parts to the operation to replace a hip joint—attaching the new "ball" to the **femur,** and replacing the socket of the **pelvic girdle.** Doctors first **dislocate** the hip so that they can work on the joint. The top of the femur is removed, and the socket in the pelvis is carved out until it is exactly the right shape to hold the new shell. Once the shape is right, the shell may be held in place by the tightness of the fit, by screws, or by special cement. A hole is then drilled into the femur, and the shaft that holds the new ball is inserted. This too can be held by its tight fit, by screws, or by cement. The metal ball is attached to the shaft, and the joint is reassembled.

After an operation

Patients are usually encouraged to start moving around again soon after a joint replacement. Doctors may use a CPM (constant passive motion) device after a knee replacement. This motorized apparatus moves the joint continuously, even while the patient is asleep, without requiring any effort from the patient. Use of a CPM can speed up the healing process considerably.

The full range of movement may not be possible with a replacement joint, but there is usually more movement and less pain than with a severely arthritic joint. Patients are advised to carry on with as many normal everyday activities as they can, but to avoid vigorous sports such as tennis and jogging.

Most replacement hips, knees, and shoulders last for ten to fifteen years. Gradually, the parts wear loose in the bones, and the person begins to feel pain while moving. Another operation is then needed, either to insert another replacement joint or to modify the existing joint to make it fit more tightly into the bone.

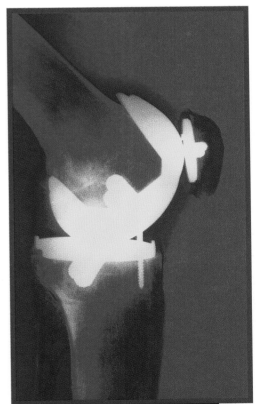

This X-ray shows the leg bones with an artificial knee joint in place.

29

The spine, or vertebral column, provides a vertical support for the upper body. It is made up of a stack of small bones, the **vertebrae,** piled one on top of another. The bony canal that runs through the vertebrae provides a protective tube for the nerves of the **spinal cord.**

The vertebral column contains 33 vertebrae, but some of them are fused together. Each single vertebra is a very slightly different shape from the ones above and below. They fit together to make a flexible column that allows us to twist around, and to bend backward, forward, and from side to side. When we stand normally, the spine curves gently in and out to absorb shock, to increase its strength, and to ensure that the body weight is distributed evenly.

The vertebral column

The vertebrae are usually thought of in separate groups:

- **cervical:** The top seven vertebrae make up the neck. The first vertebra (the "atlas") supports the head, and the joint between the atlas and the skull allows the head to nod up and down. The pivot joint between the atlas and the second vertebra (the "axis") allows the head to turn from side to side.
- **thoracic:** The next twelve vertebrae form the back of the chest. These increase in size from highest to lowest. Each thoracic vertebra is attached to a pair of ribs.
- **lumbar:** The five lumbar vertebrae are the biggest and strongest. They lie between the chest and the **pelvic girdle,** and they support the powerful muscles of the lower back.
- **sacral:** The five sacral vertebrae are separate in children but gradually fuse together during the teen and early adult years to make one strong, curved bone, the **sacrum.** This adds strength to the pelvic girdle and helps to keep it stable.
- **coccyx:** The last four (sometimes five) vertebrae also fuse together to make the coccyx, a tiny tailbone at the base of the spine.

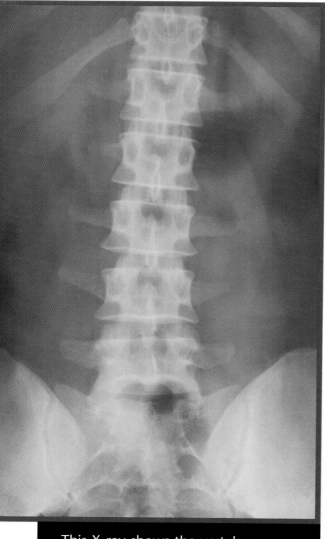

This X-ray shows the vertebrae that make up the spine.

What is a vertebra like?

Although each vertebra is different, they all follow the same basic design. The "body" is the solid front part of a vertebra. It faces inward, and it is this part that carries the weight of the rest of the body.

Seven pieces of bone, called "processes," jut out of the back and sides of the vertebral body. The spinous process and two transverse processes are sites where muscles attach. The four articular processes link directly to the vertebrae above and below, stopping the bone from slipping out of place. Together, these pieces form a bony ring, with the body of the vertebra at the front and the other pieces of bone arranged into the vertebral arch.

Protecting nerves

When the vertebrae are stacked one on top of the other, the individual bony rings line up to make a hollow column. The spinal cord is a bundle of nerves running through this channel from the base of the vertebral column to the brain. Nerves in between the vertebrae connect parts of the body with the spinal cord. The spinal cord is vitally important, carrying messages back and forth between the brain and every part of the body. Damage to the spinal cord can result in **paralysis** and loss of function, so the protection offered by the bony column of the spine is extremely important.

Disks

Between each two vertebrae is a disk of **cartilage.** The disks act as cushions to absorb shock. They also allow movement and protect the bones by stopping the vertebrae from rubbing together.

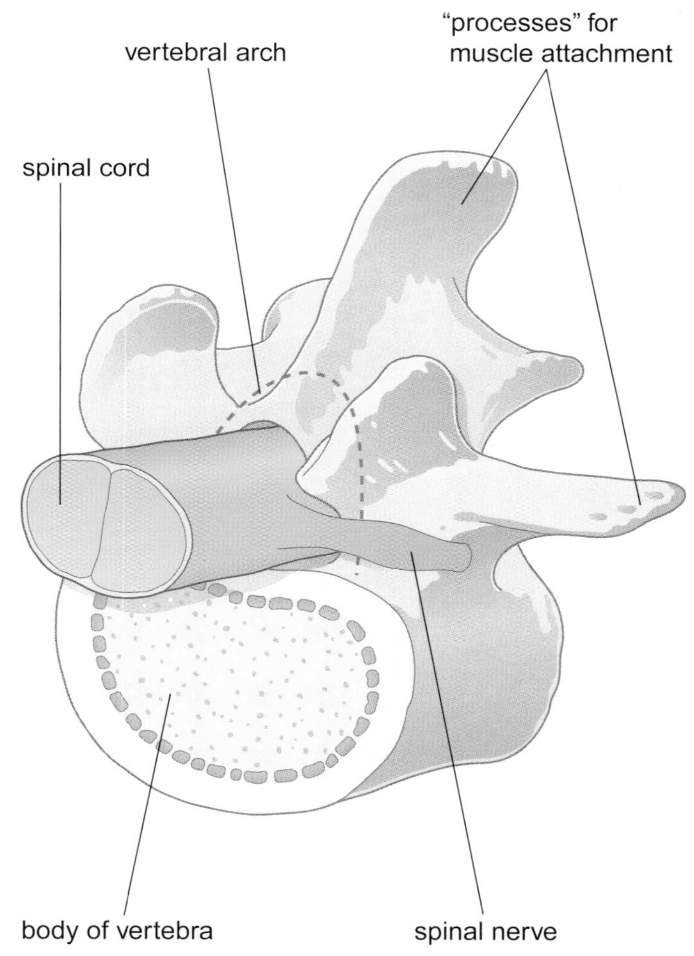

vertebral arch

"processes" for muscle attachment

spinal cord

body of vertebra

spinal nerve

This picture shows the structure of one vertebra. You can see the space that the spinal cord passes through.

TAKING CARE OF YOUR SPINE

Our spines allow us to carry out a wide range of activities, yet many of the things people do every day may be causing damage to their spines without their realizing it. The information on these pages may help you to take better care of your spine.

Carrying

The natural curves of the spine balance the body evenly, keeping the hips and shoulders more or less horizontal and making sure the weight is evenly distributed.

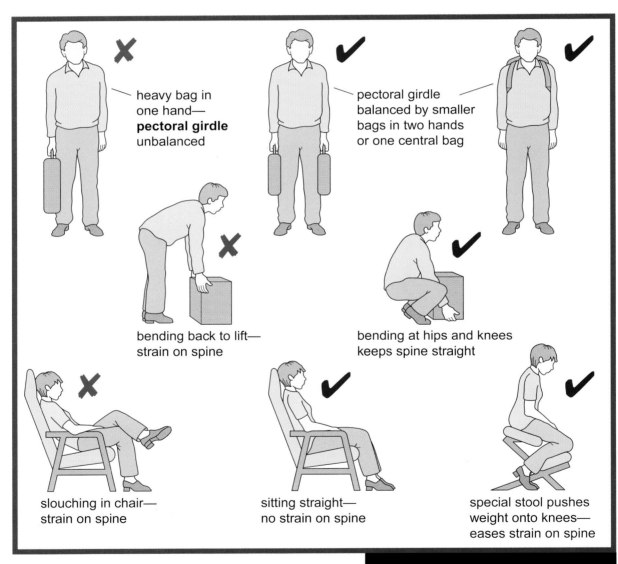

heavy bag in one hand—
pectoral girdle unbalanced

pectoral girdle balanced by smaller bags in two hands or one central bag

bending back to lift—
strain on spine

bending at hips and knees keeps spine straight

slouching in chair—
strain on spine

sitting straight—
no strain on spine

special stool pushes weight onto knees—
eases strain on spine

These diagrams show some ways to do things that can help take care of your spine.

Carrying a heavy bag on one shoulder, or in one hand, can completely distort the body's regular balance. The weight pulls down on one side, and the other side rises to compensate.

You can avoid this problem and still carry the same weight, either by sharing the load between two smaller bags—one for each hand—or by carrying it all in one central bag like a backpack. The backpack must be worn properly, with a strap over each shoulder, to distribute the weight evenly on the body.

Bending and lifting

If you curve your spine to reach down to pick up an object, you put a tremendous strain on it. A much better way is to bend your hips and knees, picking the object up with your spine as straight as possible. This method minimizes the strain on the spine.

Posture

We all lounge lazily in a chair sometimes, but this puts quite a strain on your **lumbar vertebrae.** Sitting like this regularly and for long periods can lead to back pain and other problems. Try to sit far back in your chair, with your spine as close to vertical as possible, so you are sitting on your bottom and not on your lower spine.

Hunching over a desk can make your shoulders ache, and it is not good for your spine either. Try to sit with your back straight. Some special office chairs are actually designed to take the strain off the back by spreading some of it to your knees.

Sports and spines

Some sports demand more of the spine than others do. For example, a weightlifter usually wears a strong belt to provide extra support for the lumbar vertebrae, but it is important to remember that back injuries do not only happen to athletes. Anyone who does heavy lifting, such as a mover or warehouse worker, should always wear a support belt. Warming up before you begin an activity is just as important for your spine as it is for other muscles and bones. Slow, gentle stretching movements can help to prevent strains and other injuries.

Because the spine is such a complex set of bones that bears the whole weight of the body, it is hardly surprising that injuries occur. Some problems have to do with bones, but many backaches are due mainly to muscular strain—no bones are directly involved.

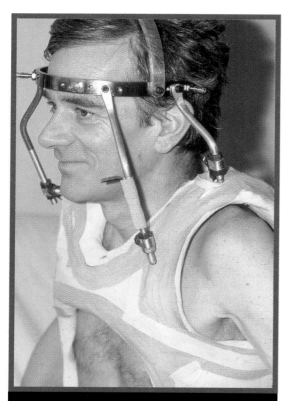

This person is wearing a neck brace to support his neck while he recovers from a spine injury.

Slipped disks

Between each two **vertebrae** is a disk of **cartilage** that acts as a shock absorber and cushion. Normally, the weight of the body pulls down evenly, squashing the disks with equal stress. Sometimes the body's weight is uneven, as when carrying a heavy weight on one side or bending a long way to one side. When this happens, the disks will be squashed unevenly, and part of a disk may jut outside the vertebral column. If this "slipped" disk presses on one of the spinal nerves, it can be extremely painful.

The treatment for a slipped disk depends on the extent of the injury. It may be enough simply to rest in bed, or gentle exercise and heat treatment may help. Traction may alleviate the problem by using a system of weights and pulleys to exert pulling forces on the spine. If the disk is badly damaged, an operation may be necessary to remove it completely and fuse the vertebrae together.

Broken back

The real danger of a "broken back" or "broken neck" is damage to the **spinal cord.** There are two main types of spinal **fractures:**
- compression fractures, where the body of one or more vertebrae is crushed. If the damage is limited to the vertebral body, and the vertebral arch is intact, the spinal cord will probably not be damaged.
- extension fractures, where the spine is pulled and stretched. An example of this is a severe whiplash injury that may be suffered in a car crash or a horse-riding fall. The neck is forced backward, the atlas vertebra breaks, and part of the axis may even be snapped. The great force can separate the skull and these two vertebrae from the rest of the spine, and may even break the spinal cord.

If the spinal cord is not damaged, a neck collar or brace may provide support. If the spinal cord is damaged, the signals along nerves to and from the brain will be interrupted. This may result in varying degrees of **paralysis** that will require long-term treatment and care.

Unusual curves

A normal spine is gently curved, but some people suffer from slightly different spinal curves.

The most common is scoliosis, where the spine curves from one side to the other, giving a twisted appearance. Much rarer is kyphosis, where the **thoracic** vertebrae are more curved than usual, giving a humped back. Lordosis, where the **lumbar** region curves forward more than usual, is also uncommon.

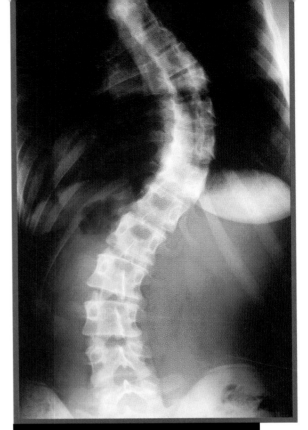

This X-ray shows the curvature of a spine affected by scoliosis.

Some babies may be born with these curvatures, and other people may develop them later as part of the aging process. They can also be caused by poor posture, obesity, or diseases such as tuberculosis (which leads to degeneration of the vertebrae) or rickets (in which the bones do not form properly).

Spina bifida

During the months before birth, the vertebral arches are open, but they gradually close around the spinal cord, enclosing it completely. In babies with spina bifida, the vertebral arches do not all close completely, and the baby is born with part of the spinal cord jutting out through the skin, covered with just a thin **membrane**. This means that the spinal cord—the vital bundle of nerves that is usually protected by the spine—could easily be damaged or infected. In some babies with spina bifida, surgery may be needed to close the gap. In others, healing may occur naturally during the first few months of life. However, many babies born with spina bifida do not survive very long. There is evidence to suggest that a mother who takes folic acid tablets during early pregnancy significantly reduces the risk of her baby having spina bifida.

SKULL

The 22 bones of the skull form a bony shell that protects the brain, eyes, and ears. They are all fixed in place except for the lower jawbone, or mandible, which is held in place by strong muscles that also help it to move. The skull bones are usually thought of in two sets: the cranial bones make up the rounded, hollow part of the head, and the facial bones make up the face.

Cranial bones

There are eight cranial bones, all joined together like a complicated jigsaw puzzle. The zigzag shapes of some of the bones makes them fit very tightly together. The joints between them, called sutures, are fixed joints, knitted together by strong fibers. Small sutural bones may occur between the sutures.

The cranial bones are:
- one frontal bone—its domed shape forms the shell of the forehead and the tops of the eye sockets
- two parietal bones—these form the top of the head and the sides above the ears
- occipital bone—this forms the lower back part of the **cranium**
- two temporal bones—there is one at each side, behind the ears
- sphenoid bone—shaped like a bat with its wings stretched out, this bone lies in front of the ears and stretches across the inside of the head from one side to the other. It helps to hold all the other cranial bones together.
- ethmoid bone—this forms internal parts of the head, like the roof of the nasal cavity.

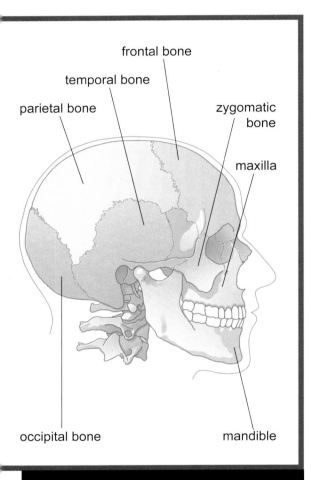

This diagram shows how some of the cranial and facial bones fit together.

Facial bones

There are fourteen irregular facial bones, which all fit together to make the complex shape of the face. The most obvious bones are the zygomatic bones (cheekbones), the nasal bones that form the bridge of the nose, and the maxillae (upper jawbones). The lower mandible (jawbone) is the largest and strongest facial bone. It forms a loose hinge with part of the temporal bones, and it can move up and down, from side to side, and backward and forward.

Sinuses

Some of the cranial and facial bones close to the nasal cavity have special hollow spaces inside them called **sinuses.** These are lined with mucus-producing **membranes,** and they drain into the nasal cavity. They act as resonating spaces, amplifying sounds when we talk and sing. **Inflammation** of the sinuses—usually due to an infection or an allergic reaction—is called sinusitis. It can cause a build-up of pressure inside the sinuses, and may lead to a bad headache.

Fontanels

The skeleton of a newborn baby is soft and delicate. Gradually, **minerals** are deposited, and the bones harden and become stronger. At birth, there are small spaces between the cranial bones that allow the skull to change its size and shape to fit through the mother's birth canal. These gaps, called fontanels or "soft spots," will eventually be the sites of the suture joints, but until the bones harden and fuse, they are very vulnerable areas.

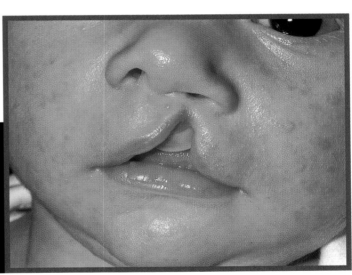

The baby in this photograph has a cleft lip and cleft palate. The two conditions often, but not always, go together.

Cleft palate and cleft lip

Usually, the maxillary bones that form the upper jaw of the face join before a baby is born. Sometimes, though, they are not properly joined at birth, and the baby has a cleft palate or a cleft lip that may affect speech and swallowing. A cleft lip is usually closed surgically just a few weeks after birth. Surgery to close a cleft palate is usually done between the ages of twelve and eighteen months, before the baby starts to talk. **Speech therapy** may be needed, but the results are usually very good.

The rib cage is made up of the ribs, the **sternum,** and the **thoracic vertebrae.** It forms a bony cage that encloses and protects the heart and lungs. Its flexibility allows the chest to expand and contract as we breathe in and out.

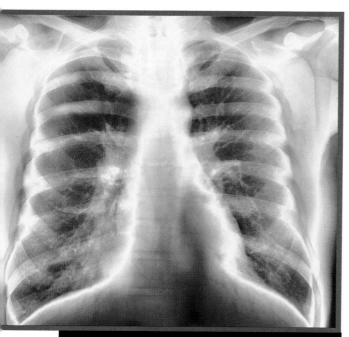

The rib cage encloses and protects the heart and lungs.

Sternum

This is a flat, dagger-shaped bone, about 6 inches (15 centimeters) long and 1.5 inches (4 centimeters) wide. It forms the center of the chest and anchors the ribs. It has three sections:

- a squarish upper section, with a notch on each side where the **clavicles** (collarbones) attach. The top pair of ribs is linked to this section, and the second pair is attached at the point where this section meets the middle section.
- a long middle section, where the rest of the ribs are attached.
- a small, pointed lower section that does not change from **cartilage** into hardened bone until the age of about 40. It provides anchorage for some major muscles.

Ribs

Most people have twelve pairs of ribs—flat bones that are curved and slightly twisted into a flattened half-circle shape. Each rib is linked at a joint to a thoracic vertebra at the back. The top seven pairs—called the "true ribs"—are joined to the sternum by strips of cartilage. The bottom five pairs are called "false ribs" because they do not connect directly to the sternum. The first three pairs of false ribs are linked to each other and to the seventh rib by strips of cartilage. The last two pairs are called "floating ribs" because they are not anchored to the sternum or to any other ribs—they are only linked to the thoracic vertebrae.

Each rib is linked to the ones above and below it by muscles that lie in the **intercostal** spaces between them. When these muscles contract, the ribs are moved upward and outward, expanding the chest space so that we can breathe in. When these muscles relax, the ribs move inward and downward, the chest space gets smaller, and we breathe out.

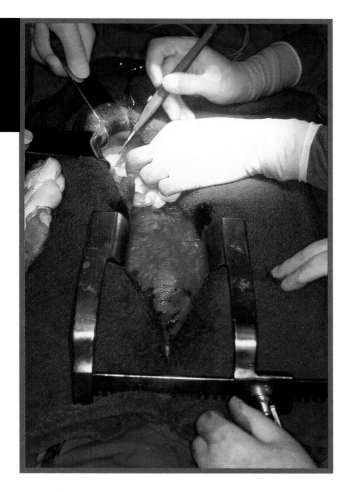

In order to perform chest surgery, such as a heart transplant, doctors must use a metal retractor to keep the ribs apart.

Broken ribs

A broken rib is the most common chest injury. It is usually the result of a heavy fall, a direct blow (such as being thrust against the steering wheel in a car accident), or pressure from a crushing weight (such as a horse landing on its rider).

The ribs tend to break where the greatest force is applied—in other words, the point where the chest was hit. They may also break at their weakest point, which is at the side of the body, where they are most curved.

Broken ribs may be very painful, but are not dangerous by themselves. However, they can lead to more serious injury if one of the **fractured** pieces damages internal organs such as the heart, lungs, liver, or **spleen.**

In many cases, cracked and broken ribs may be left to heal by themselves, sometimes with bandages around the chest to prevent further damage. In more serious cases, an operation may be necessary.

Chest surgery

If a patient needs a chest operation, such as heart surgery, doctors have to find a way to get inside the rib cage. They may do this by using a special clamp called a retractor to hold the ribs apart, and enter through the side of the rib cage. Another option is to split the sternum down the middle and open the rib cage from above. The sternum can be stitched or stapled back together after the operation.

ARM AND HAND

Our shoulder blades and collarbones form the horizontal crossbar where our arms are attached. The shoulder joint allows the upper arm to move freely in any direction. We are able to use our arms and hands to do a wide variety of different things, such as picking up heavy objects, throwing things, holding onto things, and making tiny, precise movements.

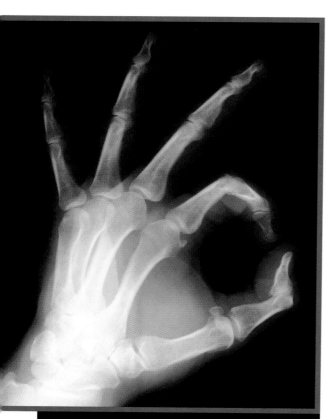

This X-ray shows the bones of the finger and thumb forming an "O." This ability to carry out tiny, precise movements is unique to humans and some other primates.

Pectoral girdle

The **scapulae** and **clavicles** together form the pectoral girdle. Each clavicle is joined to one side of the **sternum**. The shoulder blades do not join onto each other or onto the **vertebrae**. Instead, they are held in place by a complex arrangement of powerful muscles and **ligaments**.

Upper arm

The upper arm consists of a single bone, the **humerus,** which moves freely in the ball-and-socket joint with the scapula. The shaft of the humerus is roughly cylindrical, widening at the bottom into a broad, flattened triangular shape to form the top part of the elbow joint.

Elbow joint

The elbow joint is a simple hinge joint, where the humerus meets the bones of the lower arm. It allows us to bend and straighten the arm. Overuse of this joint can result in swelling and tenderness, a condition commonly known as "tennis elbow."

Lower arm

There are two bones in the lower arm—the **radius** and the **ulna.** The ulna runs from the elbow to the outside of the wrist. The radius runs from the elbow to the thumb side of the wrist. The radius and ulna meet at pivot joints at the elbow and wrist.

The radius and ulna are connected by strong fibers that lie in the space between them. These fibers allow the two bones to roll over each

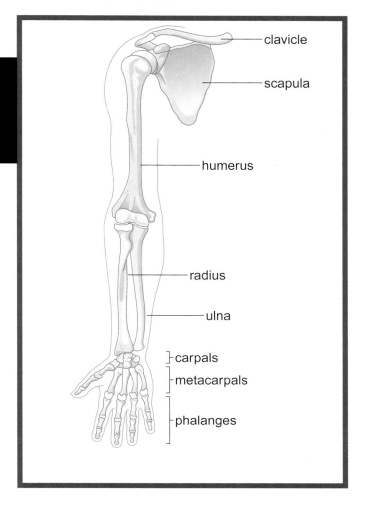

This diagram shows the bones that make up the pectoral girdle, arm, and hand.

clavicle

scapula

humerus

radius

ulna

carpals

metacarpals

phalanges

other so that we can turn our hands over from palm down to palm up and back again.

Wrist

There are eight small bones, the carpals, in each wrist. They are arranged in two rows of four bones each and are joined by ligaments. Gliding joints allow the bones to slide smoothly over each other, giving the wrist its suppleness.

Hand

The flat part of the hand is made up of five long, thin **metacarpal** bones. These are linked directly to the finger bones, the **phalanges.** Each finger has three phalanges, while the thumb has only two.

We can move each finger bone up and down to bend our fingers. The special saddle joint between the first bone of the thumb and the metacarpal allows us to move the thumb in every direction.

Carpal tunnel syndrome

The carpal bones and fibrous **tissue** together make a channel called the carpal tunnel. A bundle of long **tendons** and nerves runs through this channel. If this becomes **inflamed**, the nerves can get squashed, causing pain and tingling, and making it hard to carry out small, delicate movements. This is carpal tunnel syndrome, and it is most common in people who use their fingers a lot, such as pianists or computer operators. Treatment usually includes rest and anti-inflammatory drugs, although an operation may sometimes be necessary.

LEG AND FOOT

The structure of the leg and foot is similar to that of the arm and hand. The **pelvic girdle** provides the horizontal crossbar where the legs are attached at the hip joints. The bones of the legs are very strong, since they have to carry the weight of the whole body. The feet are flexible, allowing us to walk, run, and jump.

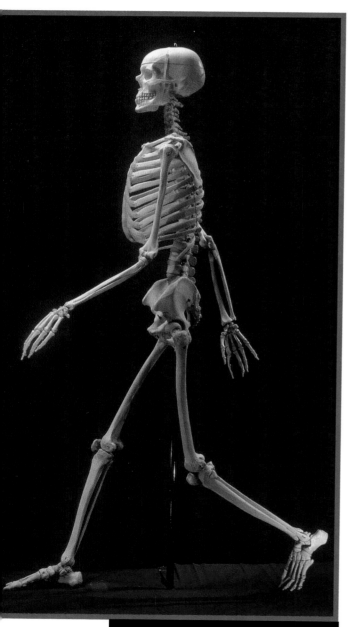

When we walk, muscles pull the bones in a carefully coordinated sequence.

Pelvic girdle

The pelvic girdle is made up of the hip bones, the **sacrum**, and the **coccyx.** The hip bones are the broadest bones in the body, and they are made up from three smaller bones—the ilium, ischium, and pubis—which fuse together during the teen and young adult years. The pelvis provides attachment sites for large muscles and for the legs, and it allows the transfer of weight between the legs and spine. It also supports and protects organs in the lower abdomen.

There are important differences between the pelvic girdles of men and women. A man's pelvis is larger and rounder than that of a woman. A woman's pelvis is wider and shallower, with a large opening to allow a baby to pass through when it is being born. These differences are valuable in helping archaeologists determine the sex of ancient skeletons.

Thigh

The thigh has a single bone, the **femur.** This is the heaviest, longest, and strongest bone in the human body. It is usually roughly one-quarter of the full height of an adult. It is attached to the pelvis by the ball-and-socket joint at the hip. The joint allows movement in all directions, but the extent of movement is strictly limited by very strong **ligaments** that prevent **dislocation.**

Knee joint

The thigh and lower leg join at the knee. The knee is a hinge joint that allows us to move the lower leg back and forth. A sesamoid bone, the **patella,** lies at the front of the knee joint.

Lower leg and foot

There are two bones in the lower leg, the **tibia** and the **fibula.** They are connected by strong fibers that allow the bones to rotate around each other. The tibia, on the inside of the leg, is the larger and stronger of the two bones, and supports the body weight. The smaller, weaker fibula, on the outside of the leg, takes little of the body weight, but it does give strength to the ankle joint.

The tibia and fibula meet the talus (ankle bone) at a hinge joint at the top of the foot. The talus fits into the calcaneus (heel bone), which lies underneath it and supports it. Together with five more bones, the **tarsals,** these bear the weight of the body. The talus acts as a lever, with major muscles attached to it by the Achilles tendon.

The long central part of the foot is made up from five **metatarsal** bones, and these are attached to the **phalanges** in the toes. The arrangement of bones is similar to that in the hands, but the bones are more restricted and have much less freedom of movement than in the hands.

Most adult feet have arches. However, if the ligaments in the foot are weak, the bones may move apart. The talus drops down into the space, and the shape of the arch collapses. This can usually be corrected by wearing a specially shaped insert (an orthotic) inside the shoe to support the bones.

Healthy bones

The bones of your legs and feet support the rest of your body and allow you to move around. As with the other bones in your body, you can help to keep them strong and healthy by exercising and eating a healthy diet. Protecting the bones makes sense too—wearing leg pads for sports like soccer and hockey can help to avoid injuries.

Shock absorbers

The tarsals and metatarsals are arranged in an arch shape, keeping us stable when we stand. This arch also allows the foot to absorb shock when we walk and run. A running step may flatten the arch by 0.4 to 0.8 inch (1 to 2 centimeters), but it springs back into shape when the pressure is released.

WHAT CAN GO WRONG WITH MY BONES?

This book has explained the different parts of the human skeleton, telling why it is important and how it can be damaged by injury and illness. These pages summarize some of the problems that can affect young people and give you information about how each is treated.

Many problems can also be avoided by good health behavior. This is called prevention. Exercising regularly and getting plenty of rest are important, as is eating a balanced diet. This is especially true in your teenage years, when your body is still developing. The table tells you some of the ways you can prevent injury and illness.

Remember, if you think something is wrong with your body, you should always talk to a trained medical professional, like a doctor or school nurse. Regular medical checkups are an important part of maintaining a healthy body.

Illness or injury	Cause	Symptoms	Prevention	Treatment
Carpal tunnel syndrome	**Inflammation** due to overuse and repetitive strain on the wrist.	Pain; tingling of fingers; inability to make precise movements with the hand.	Maintain good posture and hand position; vary activities and take breaks frequently.	Wear a **splint**. **Steroids** can reduce inflammation. Severe cases may need surgery.
Dislocation	A fall or hard impact.	A bone moves out of position in a joint.	Move with caution; don't catch yourself awkwardly when you fall.	Doctors can reposition the bones; then complete rest is needed.
Osteoarthritis	**Cartilage** is worn away by overusing joints or playing when hurt.	Joints are very painful when moved.	Don't push your body too hard; avoid use of anabolic steroids.	Drugs and rest can reduce inflammation; physiotherapy can strengthen joints.
Rickets	Lack of **vitamin** D and calcium keeps new bone from being made.	Bones become weak and may bend under even slight strain.	Eat a balanced diet that is rich in sources of calcium and vitamin D.	Change of diet to include more calcium and vitamin D.

Illness or injury	Cause	Symptoms	Prevention	Treatment
"Runner's knee"	Overuse of joint; hard or uneven surface; poor shoes; too little warmup.	Tenderness and aching under **patella.**	Warm up before activity; don't do too much; run on an even surface; wear good quality shoes.	Drugs and rest can reduce inflammation. Wearing a brace on the knee can provide relief.
Spina bifida	Incomplete closure of the **vertebral** arches at birth.	Spinal cord juts through skin, exposing nerves to damage and infection.	Pregnant women should take folic acid tablets or eat foods rich in it.	Surgery is usually required; occasionally the problem heals on its own.
Spinal problems and back pain	Poor posture when standing or sitting; carrying unbalanced loads; lifting heavy objects.	Muscle aches; weakened **ligaments**; marked curving of the spine in severe cases.	Stand and sit up straight. Bend at the knees when lifting heavy objects.	Improved posture and exercise; careful lifting and carrying.
Sprained joints	Joint gets overstretched or twisted too far out of position.	Joint is sore and is unable to bear any pressure.	Warm up before starting any exercise activity.	Rest the joint; apply ice to reduce swelling.
Stress **fractures**	Repeated use puts too much pressure on certain bones.	Sharp pain in the bone, especially in ones that bear weight.	Warm up before activity; vary movements; wear good quality shoes.	Rest is needed but can take months. Exercise is allowed if not weight-bearing.

Further Reading

Gilbert, Laura. *The Skeletal System.* New York: The Rosen Publishing Group, Inc., 2000.

Johansson, Philip. *Carpal Tunnel Syndrome and Other Repetitive Strain Injuries.* Berkeley Heights, N.J.:Enslow Publishers, Incorporated, 1999.

Llamas, Andreu. *Muscles and Bones.* Milwaukee: Gareth Stevens, Incorporated, 1998.

# GLOSSARY

abscess small area of pus surrounded by inflamed tissue

antibiotic drug used to destroy harmful bacteria and fungi

bacterium (plural is **bacteria**) microorganism that can cause infection

bone marrow soft tissue at the center of some bones, where blood cells may be produced or fat may be stored

bursa soft sac inside some joints that acts as a shock absorber

cancerous having to do with cancer

carpal wrist bone

cartilage strong, flexible material that protects bones

cervical having to do with the neck

clavicle collarbone

coccyx tailbone

compact bone strong, hard material that forms part of a bone

cranium dome of the skull

dislocate to move a bone out of its normal position

femur thigh bone

fibula smaller of the two bones of the lower leg

fracture to break a bone

friction force that occurs when two surfaces rub together

gene part of a cell that contains information related to the passing of characteristics from one generation to the next

hormone chemical made in the body that travels around the body and affects organs and tissues in a variety of ways

humerus bone of the upper arm

immune system body's natural defense mechanism against infection and disease

inflammation swelling and tenderness of a joint or other tissue

intercostal between the ribs

ligament strong band of fibers that holds a joint together

lumbar having to do with the lower back

mass amount of material that something is made of

membrane thin covering layer of tissue

metacarpal bone of the hand between the carpals and the phalanges

metatarsal bone of the foot between the tarsals and the phalanges

microorganism tiny living thing that can be seen only under a microscope

mineral one of a number of chemicals needed by the body in small amounts

occupational therapist person who helps a patient to recover after injury or illness by using suitable exercises

orthopedic relating to or specializing in bones and joints

osteoblast cell that is involved in formation of bone tissue

osteoclast cell that breaks down bone tissue

osteocyte bone cell

paralysis inability to move part of the body

patella (plural is **patellae**) kneecap

pectoral girdle framework formed by the scapulae and clavicles

pelvic girdle framework formed by the hip bones, sacrum, and coccyx

phalanx (plural is **phalanges**) bone of a finger or toe

protein type of large molecule that makes up some of the basic structures of all living things

radius bone on the thumb side of the lower arm

sacral having to do with the sacrum

sacrum fused vertebrae that form the back of the pelvic girdle

scapula (plural is **scapulae**) shoulder blade

sinus hollow space inside a cranial or facial bone

speech therapy treatment to help people with speech and language problems

spinal cord bundle of nerves that runs within the spinal column

spleen large abdominal organ involved in the formation and destruction of blood cells

splint rigid frame used to support and immobilize an injured bone

spongy bone meshlike tissue structure at the center of some bones

sternum breastbone

steroid one of a class of drugs that may be used for a variety of reasons, including reduction of inflammation

tarsal foot bone that makes up part of the ankle area

tendon strong fiber that connects muscle to bone

thoracic having to do with the chest

tibia larger of the two shin bones

tissue mass of cells that work together to do one job

tumor mass of tissue caused by abnormal growth of new cells

ulna bone on the little-finger side of the lower arm

vertebra (plural is **vertebrae**) one of the bones of the spine

vitamin one of a number of complex chemicals that the body needs in very small amounts

INDEX